W9-BWF-325

## DATE DUE

|  |  |  |  |
|--|--|--|--|
|  |  |  |  |
|  |  |  |  |
|  |  |  |  |
|  |  |  |  |
|  |  |  |  |
|  |  |  |  |
|  |  |  |  |
|  |  |  |  |
|  |  |  |  |
|  |  |  |  |
|  |  |  |  |
|  |  |  |  |
|  |  |  |  |

# Adolf HITLER

## DAVID TAYLOR

Heinemann Library
Chicago, Illinois

Customer Service 888-454-2279

Visit our website at www.heinemannlibrary.com

Designed by AMR
Illustrated by Art Construction
Originated by Dot Gradations
Printed in China

05 04 03 02 01
10 9 8 7 6 5 4 3 2 1

**Library of Congress Cataloging-in-Publication Data**
Taylor, David.
    Adolf Hitler / David Taylor.
        p. cm. --  (Leading lives)
    Includes bibliographical references and index.
    ISBN 1-58810-162-2
    1. Hitler, Adolf, 1889-1945--Juvenile literature. 2.  Heads of
    state--Germany--Biography--Juvenile literature. 3.
    Germany--History--1933-1945--Juvenile literature. 4.  National
    socialism--Juvenile literature. [1. Hitler, Adolf, 1889-1945. 2. Heads
    of state. 3. National socialism. 4. Germany--History--1933-1945.]  I.
    Title. II. Series.

DD247.H5 T353 2001
943.086'092--dc21
                                                            00-012837

**Acknowledgments**
The publishers would like to thank the following for permission to reproduce photographs:
AKG, pp. 28, 40, 49; Heinrich Hoffman/AKG, p. 26; Allsport, p. 33; Hulton Getty, pp. 4, 6 (both), 7, 15, 19, 37, 38, 43, 45, 47, 53, 55; Heinrich Hoffman/Hulton Getty, p. 10; Mary Evans Photo Library, p. 25; Popperfoto, pp. 8, 17, 23, 30, 35, 50; Süddeutscher Verlag, pp. 21, 23.

Cover photograph reproduced with permission of Corbis.

Our thanks to Christopher Gibb for his comments in the preparation of this book.

Every effort has been made to contact copyright holders of any material reproduced in this book. Any omissions will be rectified in subsequent printings if notice is given to the publishers.

Some words are shown in bold, **like this.** You can find out what they mean by looking in the glossary.

# Contents

# 1 From Hero to Zero

Adolf Hitler, the leader of the Nazi Party, became the chancellor (president) of Germany in 1933 and then proceeded to establish himself as the **dictator** of the country. He persuaded the German people that he was their savior: he was the person who would destroy the hated **Treaty of Versailles** and make Germany great once more. He also promised to lead Germany out of the **Great Depression** by strengthening the economy, ending unemployment, and creating prosperity.

Millions of Germans believed what he told them and were convinced he would deliver his promises. At the height of his popularity in the late 1930s, photographs portrayed Hitler as a caring and confident person who had many admirers.

▲ *A young admirer presented Adolf Hitler with a bunch of flowers. Hitler is wearing a swastika, the symbol of the Nazi Party, on his arm.*

In reality, Hitler was an insecure person, but he also had a "chip on his shoulder." August Kubizek, who knew him well, said, "Hitler would fly into a temper at the slightest thing . . . He was at odds with the world. Wherever he looked he saw . . . hate and enmity." Hitler was also self-conscious about his small stature and grew a moustache in an attempt to hide what he felt was his rather large nose. Before giving a speech he would practice for hours in front of a mirror to make sure he looked the part.

Hitler presided over one of the most evil governments in history, taking away the freedoms of the German people and totally controlling their lives. Anyone who opposed him was imprisoned or executed. He flooded the nation with **propaganda** to get people to believe his ideas. His attempt to create a German "master race" led directly to the murder of over 6 million Jews, gypsies, and disabled people. His foreign policy led directly to the outbreak of World War II, resulting in catastrophic loss of life and political upheaval across Europe.

Who was Adolf Hitler, what was his background, how was he able to come to power, and what has his impact been on world history? This book addresses these questions about a man whose very image is arguably the most despised of the twentieth century.

## In denial?

*"It is untrue that I . . . wanted war in 1939. It was wanted and provoked by those international statesmen who were either of Jewish descent or worked for Jewish interests . . . They are the people we have to thank for all of this."*

(Hitler's last will and testament, April 28, 1945)

# The Formative Years

Adolf Hitler was born on April 20, 1889, in the town of Braunau-am-Inn in Austria, close to the German border. He was the fourth child of Alois and Klara Hitler.

▲ *This is Klara and Alois, Hitler's parents.*

Alois worked as a customs official for the Austrian government. He was a stern, cold man and his marriage to Klara was not a happy one. Out of their six children only two, Adolf and Paula, survived into adulthood.

## The Hitler family

Alois Hitler (1837–1903) married Klara Polz (1860–1907)

| Gustav | Ida | Otto | Adolf | Edmund | Paula |
|---|---|---|---|---|---|
| (1885–87) | (1886–88) | (born 1887) | (1889–1945) | (1894–1900) | (1896–1960) |
| [died from diphtheria] | [died from measles] | [died a few days old] | | | |

## School days

Adolf did well at primary school, but when he transferred to the **Realschule** in 1900, in the nearby town of Linz, his attitude changed. He developed a streak of arrogance and became lazy and sullen. The only subjects that interested him were history and art. Alois Hitler, a strict disciplinarian, showed his displeasure by beating his wayward son. In contrast, Klara spoiled Adolf and showered him with love and affection, probably because he was her first child to survive infancy.

▲ *This school photograph of Hitler was taken in 1899, when he was ten.*

Alois died in 1903. Free of his controlling father, Adolf persuaded his mother to let him leave school early in 1905. He was too lazy to find a job, and idled his time away at home reading, sketching, and fantasizing about the future. He dreamt that he was destined to become a famous artist. Hitler's only friend was August Kubizek, a promising musician.

## Hitler moves to Vienna

In September 1907, at the age of eighteen, Hitler went to live in Vienna. He applied to be a student at the Vienna Academy of Art but was rejected. Hitler's pride was severely dented, and he later said that his rejection was "like a bolt from the blue." On learning that his mother was terminally ill with cancer, Hitler returned to Linz. He was deeply saddened when she died on December 21, 1907.

◄ *Hitler did this painting of the Karlskirche in Vienna while he was staying in a shelter for the homeless.*

Hitler returned to Vienna in February 1908, accompanied by Kubizek, who studied at the music academy. Since Hitler had an orphan's pension, he did not have to get a job, and he roamed the streets admiring the fine architecture. In the summer of 1908, Hitler submitted a second application to study at the Academy of Art but was again turned down. Too ashamed to tell Kubizek of this second failure, he moved out of the apartment they were sharing and found cheaper lodgings on his own. By 1909, he had run out of money and was forced to sleep on the streets. When the winter came, Hitler found shelter in a home for tramps. His fortunes, however, improved when an aunt sent him some money, enabling him to move to a more comfortable hostel. By this time Hitler had met Reinhold Hanisch, a street-wise wanderer and petty criminal. Hanisch was impressed by Hitler's artistic talent and persuaded him to paint postcards with scenes of Vienna. Hanisch then sold the postcards on the streets, earning the two men enough money to live on.

## Hitler's "world picture" takes shape

Hitler claimed that his experiences in Vienna gave him a "world picture" and shaped his political thinking. Vienna, a city of over 1.5 million people, was the capital of the huge Austro-Hungarian Empire, which contained a wide mix of **ethnic groups,** including Germans, Poles, Czechs, Slovaks, and Serbs. The German-speaking Hitler disliked the other groups, and felt that the Germans were a superior race. He was a staunch German **nationalist,** believing that all German people in Europe should join together and live in one country.

## Anti-Semitism

Anti-Semitism is a phrase used to describe the persecution of Jews and feelings of hatred toward them. In 70 A.D., the Romans expelled the Jews from Palestine and they were forced to settle in various parts of Europe. Many Jews became successful traders, and some other people grew to resent this. During the nineteenth century anti-Semitism was common in Austria, France, Germany, Poland, and Russia, causing many Jewish people to move to the U.S. In 1896, Theodore Herzl, a Hungarian Jew living in Vienna, published a pamphlet in which he said the Jews should be allowed to return to Palestine.

Vienna was also the home of 175,000 Jewish people. Many of them were wealthy teachers, businesspeople, and lawyers who lived in large houses. Hitler resented their success and started to read **scurrilous** anti-Jewish magazines. He persuaded himself that the Jews were to blame for the problems of the world. Hitler also encountered **communists** in Vienna, and he disagreed strongly with their belief that all people should be equal. To Hitler, some people were naturally entitled to more than others. Already Hitler's prejudiced opinions were well formed.

# Hitler and World War I

In May 1913, Hitler moved to Munich, the capital of the **state** of Bavaria in southern Germany. Here he continued to make a meager living by painting postcards. At the beginning of 1914, he was summoned to Austria to explain why he had not registered for the army. Hitler hated the thought of serving in the Austrian army and told the military **tribunal** he was not fit enough for service. He was allowed to go free and return to Munich.

## Hitler joins the German army

When World War I broke out on August 1, 1914, Hitler immediately volunteered to join the German army. He was accepted by the 16th Bavarian Infantry Regiment and served on the **Western Front** as a motorbike message runner. The war gave Hitler the sense of purpose that was so badly missing from his life at the time.

▲ A huge crowd, including an enthusiastic Hitler, turned out in the Odeonplatz in Munich on August 2, 1914, to celebrate the outbreak of World War I.

In December 1914, Hitler was awarded the Iron Cross, Second Class, for bravery. Many of his colleagues, however, regarded him as quite strange since he always volunteered for extra duties. In 1916, Hitler was wounded in the thigh and was away from the front line for five months. After he returned in July 1918, he delivered a vital message, despite being under heavy fire. For this he was awarded the Iron Cross, First Class. Then, in October 1918, he was partially blinded by mustard gas and taken to a hospital to recover.

## Germany defeated

By now the German generals knew they were beaten and advised the government to ask for peace. The army was being pushed back and suffering heavy casualties. Within Germany there were naval **mutinies** and food was in short supply. People were tired of the war. On November 9, the German kaiser (emperor), Wilhelm II, was forced to abdicate and flee to the Netherlands. A new democratic government, the **Weimar** Republic, was declared and on November 11, the new government signed the **armistice.** Germany had lost the war.

## Organization of the Weimar Republic

The new German government took its name from the town of Weimar, where it first met in early 1919.

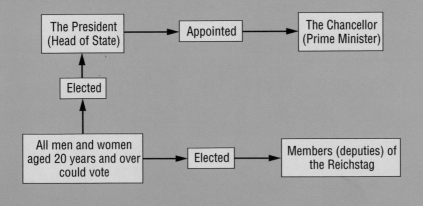

Hitler was still in the hospital when he heard the news of Germany's defeat. He was furious and asked himself if the war had been fought "so that a gang of wretched criminals [the leaders of the new German democratic government] could lay their hands on the Fatherland." Hitler was convinced that the army could have gone on fighting but believed Jews, **communists,** and democratic politicians had plotted to take Germany out of the war. He returned to his army barracks in Munich wondering what the future would bring.

### Vengeance for the German nation!

*"Today in the Hall of Mirrors at Versailles a disgraceful treaty is being signed. Never forget it! . . . There will be vengeance for the shame of 1919."*

(Headlines from the *Deutsche Zeitung,* a German newspaper, June 28, 1919)

## The Treaty of Versailles

There was chaos in Germany following the end of World War I. In January 1919, communists tried to seize control of the country, but the army crushed the uprising. Some Germans wanted a return to the old style of government and to be ruled by the kaiser once more. On June 28, 1919, Germany signed the **Treaty of Versailles.** The Germans had not been allowed to negotiate the terms of the treaty, so Hitler called it a *diktat* (a dictated peace). The treaty made Germany take sole responsibility for causing World War I and ordered Germany to pay $33 billion in reparations (war damages). Hitler said the treaty was humiliating and a national disgrace. To add insult to injury, when a new international peacekeeping organization, the **League of Nations,** was formed in 1920, Germany was not allowed to join. All of this was too much for many Germans, including Hitler, who now decided to turn to politics to overturn the **Weimar** government.

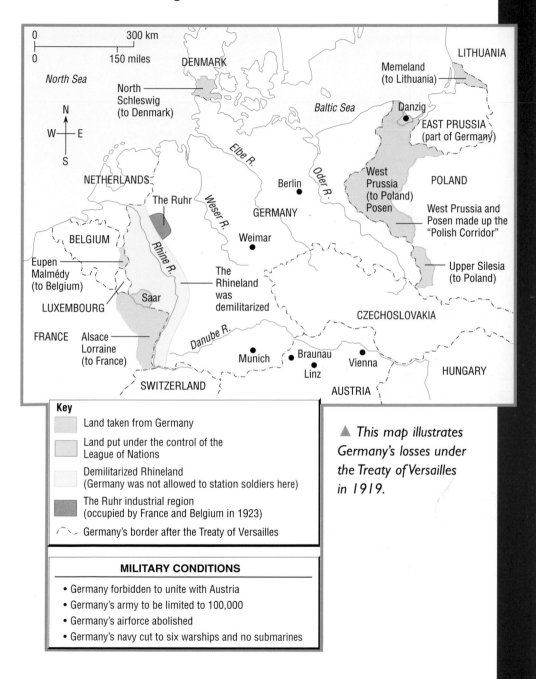

▲ *This map illustrates Germany's losses under the Treaty of Versailles in 1919.*

**Key**

- Land taken from Germany
- Land put under the control of the League of Nations
- Demilitarized Rhineland (Germany was not allowed to station soldiers here)
- The Ruhr industrial region (occupied by France and Belgium in 1923)
- Germany's border after the Treaty of Versailles

---

**MILITARY CONDITIONS**

- Germany forbidden to unite with Austria
- Germany's army to be limited to 100,000
- Germany's airforce abolished
- Germany's navy cut to six warships and no submarines

# Hitler Enters the Political Arena

In January 1919, a locksmith named Anton Drexler set up a small political group in Munich called the German Workers' Party (*Deutsche Arbeiterpartei* or DAP). He wanted to help the ordinary workers and restore Germany to its former glory. On September 12, 1919, the German army authorities sent Hitler to a Munich beer hall to speak to the DAP about the evils of **Communism.** Hitler made a fiery and fanatical speech, which so impressed Drexler that he invited Hitler to join the party as a committee member. After some thought, Hitler accepted and became the party's 55th member.

## The birth of the Nazi Party

Hitler was put in charge of **propaganda** and given the task of advertising the party's opinions and arranging meetings to "spread the word." On February 24, 1920, a meeting attended by 2,000 people was held in the Hofbrauhaus beer hall in Munich. Here Hitler and Drexler announced a 25-point program that outlined the objectives of the DAP.

### Extracts from the 25-point program

We, the German Workers' Party, demand the following:

1  The union of all German-speaking people in Europe into a Greater Germany
2  The abolition of the **Treaty of Versailles**
3  Extra living space (*lebensraum*) for the German people
4  Jews to be banned from being German citizens
. . .
14  Profit sharing in big industries
15  Adequate pensions for old people

## Hitler takes over as party leader

In April 1920, the party's name was changed to the **Nationalist** Socialist German Workers' Party (*Nationalsozialistische Deutsche Arbeiterpartei*). This was soon abbreviated to the Nazi Party. Hitler put his heart and soul into raising the party's profile and made numerous speeches in Munich and the surrounding area, attacking Jews, the **Weimar** government, and the Treaty of Versailles. He also designed the party's logo, based on the ancient swastika symbol, in black against a red and white background.

The membership of the Nazi Party began to grow and it was obvious that Hitler, rather than Drexler, was the driving force. In July 1921, there was a quarrel among the committee members of the Nazi Party. Hitler knew he was more valuable to the party than Drexler, and threatened to resign unless he was made leader. Drexler was forced to give in. The party committee was disbanded and Hitler was given total control. Anyone who challenged his authority was expelled from the party. By now he was well known in the **state** of Bavaria and had a number of close allies within the party, including Ernst Röhm, Hermann Göring, and Rudolf Hess.

▶ *Hitler was photographed here speaking in a Munich street during the early days of the Nazi Party. He had a talent for public speaking and was able to persuade people to think his way.*

## Rohm and the SA

In the autumn of 1921, the Nazis set up a trained militia group known as the SA (*Sturm Abteilung*, or storm troopers). Made up of ex-soldiers, the SA wore brown shirts and were under the leadership of Ernst Röhm. Their job was to protect party leaders and break up the meetings of rival groups, especially those held by the **communists.** Hitler said the SA made the Nazis a "political fighting force" and not just a "debating society." The Nazis were growing in strength, and by 1923 they had attracted 50,000 to their ranks.

▲ SA members paraded in a Munich square, carrying banners that said, "Germany awake!" The SA soon had a reputation for violence. They attacked and beat up political opponents in the street.

# 5 The Munich *Putsch*

By the end of 1922, the **Weimar** government was falling behind with the payment of **reparations** so, in January 1923, French and Belgian troops invaded the Ruhr, the main industrial region in Germany. At the same time, Germany was suffering from hyperinflation, which was a situation where prices rose dramatically, banknotes became worthless, and millions of people lost their savings overnight. The Weimar government was now more unpopular than ever.

## Drama in Munich

A frustrated Hitler felt that the time was right to attempt a *putsch* (seizing of power) in Germany. On the evening of November 8, 1923, Gustav von Kahr, the head of the Bavarian **state** government, was giving a speech in the Burger Bräu Keller, a beer hall in Munich. Hundreds of storm troopers surrounded the hall and Hitler burst in, firing a shot into the ceiling. He announced that the Nazis were taking over the Bavarian government, and that they would then go to Berlin to overthrow the Weimar government.

▶ *Hitler and his followers were photographed outside the Bürger Bräu Keller on November 9, 1923.*

The next day over 3,000 Nazis marched into the center of Munich, but police blocked their way and opened fire. In the resulting mayhem, sixteen Nazis and three policemen were shot dead. Hitler dislocated his shoulder in the crush. He fled the scene to a villa owned by his friend, Ernst Hanfstaengl. Hanfstaengl's wife, Helene, hid him from the police, but two days later Hitler was arrested.

## Hitler on trial

On February 26, 1924, Hitler went on trial accused of high **treason.** He defended himself effectively and argued that he had only been trying to rid Germany of a government that had betrayed the country. The trial was widely reported, and Hitler became famous throughout Germany. Hitler received the minimum sentence of five years' imprisonment. While in Landsberg Prison, Hitler used the time to dictate *Mein Kampf* (*My Struggle*), which told his life story and set out his political ambitions. It was a poorly written book that carried a chilling message. He wrote that the Germans were members of the **Aryan** race, which was superior to other people such as Jews, **Slavs,** Africans, and gypsies. According to Hitler, the Jews were the lowest race. They were, he said, responsible for all of Germany's problems and needed to be expelled from the country. There was, of course, no factual basis for these opinions. They were the ramblings of a person with deeply held prejudices. Hitler called for the abolition of the **Treaty of Versailles** and said that the German people needed more living space, which would be acquired by invading the communist **USSR.** Finally, Hitler expressed his hatred of **Communism** and **democracy,** arguing that Germany needed a strong government with decisions being made by one powerful leader.

On December 19, 1924, the Bavarian Supreme Court, sympathetic to the views of Hitler, ordered his immediate release from prison for showing excellent behavior. He was released the next day, having served just nine months of his sentence.

The failure of the Munich *putsch*, however, had taught Hitler an important lesson: if the Nazi Party was to come to power in Germany, it would have to be done legally, by winning more votes than the other political parties.

▲ *This picture of Hitler was taken by Heinrich Hoffman, his official photographer, on his release from Landsberg Prison on December 20, 1924.*

On his release from prison, Hitler set about reestablishing himself as the leader of the Nazi Party. He introduced his own personal bodyguard, known as the **SS** (*Schutzstaffel* or protection squad). Hitler also changed the way the Nazi Party was organized so that it had branches throughout Germany. The country was divided into 34 areas called *gau* (districts), each under the control of a *gauleiter* (district leader). It was the *gauleiter's* job to promote the Nazi Party in his district. In July 1926, the first party **rally** was held in **Weimar** with a gathering of over 5,000 storm troopers. It was here that the straight arm Nazi salute and the greeting *Heil Hitler* (Hail Hitler) were first used.

Germany, however, was enjoying a period of prosperity at this time. Gustav Stresemann, the foreign minister, had managed to end inflation, increase trade, and improve Germany's standing abroad. In 1926, Germany was allowed to join the **League of Nations.** When elections for the **Reichstag** were held in May 1928, the Nazis won only twelve seats.

## The Great Depression

In 1929, world trade slumped after the collapse of the U.S. **stock market** on Wall Street in New York. The world was plunged into the **Great Depression,** which lasted well into the 1930s. The American banks stopped lending money to Germany. German factories were forced to close and unemployment rose rapidly. The Weimar government seemed unable to do anything about the problem. Hitler told the German people that he would provide jobs and cure unemployment, and in the Reichstag elections of 1930, the Nazis won 107 seats.

## Geli Raubal

When Hitler wanted some peace he rented a property called the Haus Wachenfeld, near Berchtesgaden in Bavaria. The house was built on the side of a mountain and had wonderful views of the surrounding area. Hitler employed his half-sister, Angela Raubal, to be housekeeper, and she moved in with her daughter, Geli, who was twenty years old and very attractive.

▲ *This is a photograph of Geli Raubal.*

Before long Hitler had fallen in love with his niece, and the pair were frequently seen together in public. Hitler, however, was very possessive, and when Geli said she wished to go to Vienna to train as an opera singer he flew into a rage. On September 17, 1931, Hitler left for a meeting in Hamburg, and the next morning Geli was found dead. She had shot herself in the heart. At her funeral Hitler wept uncontrollably, and for months afterward he was downcast and dejected. By this time Hitler had bought the Haus Wachenfeld. He later rebuilt it into a much larger residence known as the Berghof (Mountain Hall), using it as a private retreat and conference center. Throughout Hitler's life, Geli's room was kept precisely as she had left it.

## 1932—a crucial year

In 1932, Germany was still in the grips of the **Great Depression.** Unemployment had risen to 6 million and the government was still unable to relieve the situation. In February, Hitler was granted German citizenship, and in the spring he ran against the elderly Paul von Hindenburg in the presidential elections. Hindenburg, an ex-army general, had served Germany with distinction in World War I and was a popular figure. Hitler failed to beat him but received over 13 million votes. In July, the Nazis won 230 seats in the **Reichstag** election, making them the largest single party in the Reichstag. Hitler worked tirelessly to spread the Nazi message, traveling by air to over 50 towns and cities where he made emotional speeches. He told people how the Nazis would solve unemployment, tear up the **Treaty of Versailles,** and restore Germany to its former glory. It was an attractive message to many people.

### How the Nazis profited from rising unemployment

|  | May 1928 | July 1932 |
|---|---|---|
| Unemployment | 0.8 million | 6 million |
| Nazi seats in the Reichstag | 12 | 230 |

Meanwhile, Hitler had struck up a relationship with Eva Braun, the daughter of a Munich schoolteacher. He had first met her in 1929, when she was working for Heinrich Hoffman, his official photographer. She was tall and blond and had a love of dancing and jazz. Eva moved into the Berghof, where she had her own room.

◄ *Eva Braun posed for this photograph in Heinrich Hoffman's studio in the early 1930s.*

Hitler, however, did not wish to be seen in public with her, and when visitors came she was kept out of sight. She grew unhappy at the lack of attention and on November 1, 1932, attempted suicide by shooting herself in the neck. She lived and recovered in the hospital.

In the same month the Nazis won 196 seats in another election for the Reichstag. Although this was a reduction of 34 seats, they were still the largest single party. Hitler argued that he should be appointed chancellor (president) of Germany. President Hindenburg distrusted Hitler, but on January 30, 1933, he gave in and made Hitler chancellor.

► *Hitler sat here with President Hindenburg shortly after being appointed chancellor. Hitler had come to power legally, but he soon set about destroying* **democracy** *in Germany.*

On the night of January 30, 1933, delighted Nazi Party members celebrated Hitler's appointment as chancellor by holding dramatic torchlight parades all over Germany. Hitler, however, realized his authority was limited. He was still under the control of President Hindenburg, who had the power to dismiss him at any time he wished. Hitler wanted to be the **dictator** of Germany, and he quickly set about bringing down the democratic **Weimar** government.

## The Reichstag fire

Hitler needed the Nazis to have an **overall majority** in the **Reichstag,** so he asked President Hindenburg to call an election for March 5, 1933. On February 27, 1933, the Reichstag building in Berlin mysteriously caught fire. Hitler was having dinner when he was informed. His chauffeur drove him at high speed to the scene. Hitler told Hindenburg the building had been deliberately set on fire by **communists,** who were planning an armed uprising. The SA went on the rampage, arresting and imprisoning over 4,000 communists. In the election that followed, the Nazis won 288 seats, but they still did not have an overall majority. Hitler cleverly invited the **Nationalist** Party and Center Party to join the Nazis, and together they had a majority of just sixteen seats over the other parties.

On March 23, 1933, the Reichstag **deputies** met in the Kroll Opera House in Berlin. SA men surrounded the premises and prevented the communists from taking their seats. Hitler made a long speech in which he promised to end unemployment, but said he needed more power to achieve this and asked the Reichstag to pass an act that would give him the authority to make laws on his own. The act was passed by 441 votes to 84. **Democracy** in Germany had come to an end.

▲ *The Reichstag building was still burning on the morning of February 28, 1933. Marinus van der Lubbe, a simple-minded Dutch communist, was blamed for the fire and executed in 1934.*

## Personal matters

In the summer of 1933, Hitler went to the Berghof for a vacation, accompanied by Helene Hanfstaengl and her son, Egon. On a number of occasions, prominent members of the Nazi Party joined them for dinner. Although Hitler gave his opinions on different matters at these gatherings, he always refused to talk about his family background. Rumors had been circulating in Germany around that time that Hitler's grandfather was Jewish. Although this has never been proved, Hitler obviously saw it as a matter of potential embarrassment, given his **anti-Semitic** opinions.

▲ The Berghof was Hitler's retreat in the Bavarian Alps near Berchtesgaden. Hitler enlarged the house during the mid-1930s using Nazi Party funds. Whenever he stayed at the Berghof, hundreds of tourists would gather on the mountain slopes around the house, trying to get a glimpse of him.

It was not long before Jewish people in Germany were being persecuted. On April 1, the Nazis ordered a **boycott** of Jewish shops. SA men were posted outside shop doors to prevent people from entering. It was a sign of things to come in the following years. Next, Hitler banned **trade unions,** censored the newspapers, and outlawed all the other political parties. By July 1933, the Nazis were the only legal political party left in Germany. Every deputy in the **Reichstag** was now a Nazi. Anyone who dared to oppose Hitler was arrested and imprisoned in a **concentration camp,** the first of which was set up in February 1933.

## The Night of the Long Knives

By 1934, the SA had over 3 million members. Ernst Röhm told Hitler that he wanted the army to be joined with the SA and placed under his command. This was too much for Hitler. Such a move would make Röhm extremely powerful and a threat to Hitler's authority. Hitler, in turn, needed to have the army on his side, so he decided to eliminate Röhm. This would cement his own position and gain the support of the army generals. On June 30, 1934, members of the black-shirted **SS** arrested and imprisoned Röhm. Many other leading SA members were murdered in cold blood. On July 1, Röhm was given a gun and told to shoot himself. When he refused, SS soldiers shot him. The purging of the SA became known as the "Night of the Long Knives."

A few days later Hitler attempted to justify the killings by saying there were "destructive elements" in the SA, who were "enemies" of Germany. On August 2, 1934, President Hindenburg died at the age of 87. Hitler now joined together the positions of chancellor and president and announced that he was the Führer (leader) of Germany. On the same day, the German army swore an oath of personal loyalty to Hitler, who now had complete control. The next step was to transform Germany into a Nazi state.

### The army's oath of loyalty

*"I swear by God this sacred oath, that I will render unconditional obedience to Adolf Hitler, the Führer of the German Reich [Empire] and people, Supreme Commander of the Armed Forces, and will be ready as a brave soldier to risk my life any time for this oath."*

Under the **Weimar** government, from 1919 to 1933, Germany was a democratic country. German people were free to do as they liked within the law. They could vote in elections, openly criticize the government, and join **trade unions.**

From 1933, Hitler and his Nazi government took control of all aspects of life in Germany. The **SS** and Gestapo (secret police), headed by Heinrich Himmler, used terror tactics to frighten people into obeying the Nazis. The Gestapo built up a network of informers who reported anyone who criticized Hitler or refused to give the Nazi salute. Many people were dragged from their beds in the middle of the night, brutally questioned, and sent to **concentration camps.**

### Education

The Nazi minister of education said that "the whole purpose of education [was] to create Nazis." Textbooks were rewritten so that they contained Nazi ideas. Children were required to give the Nazi salute each morning and to sing Nazi

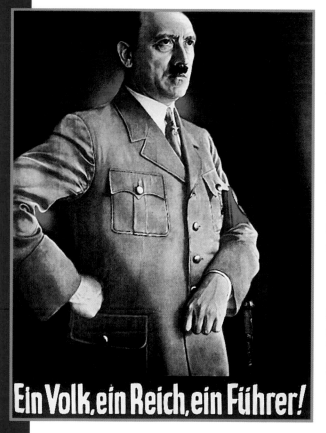

Ein Volk, ein Reich, ein Führer!

◀ *This Nazi* **propaganda** *poster portrayed Hitler as the absolute leader of Germany. The caption means "One People, One Empire, One Leader!"*

songs. They were taught about the shame of the **Treaty of Versailles** and how Hitler would restore Germany's pride. Any teachers who refused to teach Nazi ideas were dismissed and imprisoned. Starting in 1936, teenagers were required to join the **Hitler Youth,** where they played sports and had the chance to pursue a range of outdoor activities that would keep them fit and healthy. Boys were given military training and taught to hate Jews. Girls were taught that the place for women was in the home.

## Ilse Sonja Totzke

Ilse was reported to the Gestapo by her neighbors. Her "crime" was that she was too friendly with the Jewish people on her street. She was arrested by the Gestapo, sent to a concentration camp, and never heard from again.

## Persecution of the Jews

Hitler set out to create a nation of "pure" Germans who would follow him as their leader. He wanted to eliminate such groups as Jews, gypsies, and disabled people. Hitler persecuted Jewish people methodically in Germany. Jews were banned from professional jobs, such as teaching, and told they were not allowed to use cinemas, parks, public swimming pools, and restaurants. Notices reading "Jews not wanted here" and "Bathing prohibited for dogs and Jews" were found in towns throughout Germany. In September 1935, the Nazis introduced the Nuremberg Laws, which stated that Jews could not be German citizens and were forbidden to marry non-Jewish Germans. In a speech at a **rally** in the city of Nuremberg, Hitler explained that he was "purifying" the German race so that everyone had pure Germanic blood.

In early November 1938, a Jew in Paris murdered a German politician. With Hitler's knowledge, the Nazis used this as an excuse for a nationwide attack on Jewish businesses, **synagogues,** and shops. On the night of November 9–10, 1938, the fifteenth anniversary of the Munich *putsch*, Nazi mobs went on the rampage across Germany. Altogether they burned down 267 synagogues, smashed the windows of 8,000 Jewish shops, and murdered 91 Jewish people. Thousands of Jews were arrested and sent to **concentration camps.** A British reporter who was in Berlin at the time said that many "average Germans looked on, either apathetic or ashamed." The event became known as Kristallnacht (the "Night of Crystal Glass") because large amounts of broken glass littered the streets. Thousands of Jews, fearing for their safety, fled Germany.

▼ *Pedestrians walked past the damage done to a Jewish shop in Berlin following the "Night of Crystal Glass," on November 10, 1938.*

## The role of women

Hitler believed that women should stay at home and bear as many "pure" German children as possible. Women were encouraged to have large families, and the Nazis made it difficult for them to follow a career. They were expected not to wear makeup or smoke in public. Hitler's treatment of Eva Braun followed most of this pattern. He refused to marry her because he thought it would affect his work. Eva was not allowed to smoke and was kept out of view of the public. Hitler spent long periods away from her on government business in the **Chancellery** in Berlin and, in May 1935, she was so depressed that she tried to commit suicide for a second time. This time she attempted a drug overdose. Her sister found her in a coma and called a doctor, who managed to revive Eva.

### A Jewish doctor is forced to leave Germany

*"The Jewish doctor of my children . . . told me that he was going to be dismissed from his children's clinic in Hamburg, and that he had received threatening letters telling him that if he laid his hands on **Aryan** children there would be trouble. . . . I realized for the first time that something very evil was afoot [in Germany]. . . . His wife said that his heart had been broken by what had happened to him . . . He left Germany and went to Holland where he committed suicide."*

(Christabel Bielenberg, the British wife of a German lawyer, who lived in Germany during the Nazi period)

## The economy

Hitler introduced a program of public works to solve the problem of high unemployment in Germany. People were employed to build autobahns (highways), public buildings, hospitals, and schools. Starting in 1935, jobs were created in the armaments industry as Hitler ordered the manufacture of warships, guns, aircraft, and tanks. Unemployment dropped from 6 million in 1933, to less than 1 million in 1938.

The German Labor Front, established with Hitler's consent by Robert Ley, controlled both the workers and the employers. Workers were bribed to be obedient through the provision of cheap vacations and leisure activities. Hitler boasted that he had brought prosperity back to Germany, but this was far from true. Wages were deliberately kept low and hours were long. People had actually been better off in 1929.

## Propaganda

In 1933, Hitler put Joseph Goebbels in charge of **propaganda.** It was his job to make the German people believe in Nazi ideas and follow the leadership of Hitler. He used the radio to broadcast Nazi ideas, and organized impressive **rallies** to show how powerful the Nazis were. In 1934, Hitler ordered a leading film producer, Leni Riefenstahl, to make a documentary film of a rally in the city of Nuremberg. During the six days of the rally, the Nazis put on a magnificent show of strength and pageantry. On the final day of the rally, Hitler made a dramatic speech under floodlights to an audience of over 200,000. At the end of the speech, Rudolf Hess, the deputy leader of the Nazi Party, thanked Hitler and whipped the crowd into further frenzy by shouting: "Hitler is Germany just as Germany is Hitler. *Heil Hitler! Sieg*

*Heil!*" (Hail Hitler, Hail victory). Riefenstahl's film, called the
*Triumph of the Will*, captured the full drama of the occasion.
Films that ridiculed Jews were also made, with the aim of
stirring up hatred of Jewish people.

## A propaganda triumph: the 1936 Berlin Olympics

In the summer of 1936, the Olympic Games were staged in Berlin.
Here was a wonderful chance for Hitler to show the Nazis in a
good light to the world. Anti-Jewish posters were taken down and
a magnificent new stadium was built. Hitler opened the games
before a crowd of 110,000. The African-American athlete, Jesse
Owens, won four gold medals, but Hitler did not present his
medals to him as he
considered African people
to be inferior. The fact
that Germany won the
most gold, silver, and
bronze medals, however,
was highly satisfactory to
Hitler. In his eyes it
proved that the **Aryan**
race was superior to
others. Most of the
foreign visitors left
Berlin impressed with
the welcome they had
been given.

△ *Jesse Owens was photographed here
during the 1936 Olympic Games in Berlin.*

Goebbels made sure that newspapers were controlled. Any article that disagreed with the Nazis was censored. Books written by Jews and **communists** were publicly burned, as they were considered to be "un-German." On May 11, Goebbels incited students to burn 20,000 books on a huge bonfire in the center of Berlin. All new film scripts were checked to make sure they did not contain passages criticizing the Nazis. Jewish actors and directors were banned from working in the film industry. Modern artists, such as Paul Klee, who had flourished under the Weimar government, had their work banned as **"degenerate"** and "decadent." Only art that portrayed Nazi beliefs about race, the family, and war was allowed.

## Hitler's daily routine as Führer

Although the Nazi government was based in the Chancellery in Berlin, Hitler spent a lot of his time at the Berghof in Bavaria. Each day he had breakfast in bed at about 11:00 A.M., before getting up at noon. He then held discussions with his advisers and any ministers who had arrived from Berlin. He had lunch at 2:00 P.M. and, as Hitler had been a vegetarian since 1931, it consisted of potatoes, cheese, vegetable dumplings, and oatmeal. Guests, however, were provided with a variety of meat dishes. Between meals, Hitler consumed large amounts of cake and chocolate. Hitler would talk at length over lunch. People were expected to listen and agree with what he said. Late in the afternoon he took his Alsatian dog for a walk and then spent time reading before having dinner at 9:00 P.M., after which Hitler watched movies into the small hours of the morning. Among his favorites were *King Kong* and *Snow White*.

Hitler allowed his ministers to deal with the running of Germany, under the basic principles he had laid down. He often signed papers without even reading them. Despite this, his position as Führer was unchallenged. Only in matters to do with foreign policy and the armed forces did Hitler take a part in making major decisions. This was to have huge consequences, not just for Germany, but also the world.

▲ *Hitler and Eva Braun were photographed here at the Berghof. Hitler enjoyed his visits to the Berghof, where he could rest and escape the pressures of government.*

# The Road to War

Hitler knew exactly what he wanted to achieve in foreign affairs. He was determined to destroy the **Treaty of Versailles** and create a Greater Germany in which all German-speaking people would be brought together. Once this was done, the German people would need more *lebensraum,* and he aimed to get this by invading eastern Europe and the **USSR.** Taking this territory would also provide Germany with vital supplies of oil, coal, and iron ore.

## Germany rearms

At first, Hitler was very cautious. He did not want other countries to think he was a danger to peace. In his book, *Mein Kampf,* Hitler had written that "a clever conqueror will always impose his demands on the conquered by installments." In October 1933, he took Germany out of the **League of Nations,** arguing that it was unfair for other countries to be armed when Germany was not permitted to be. In January 1934, he signed a treaty with the Poles saying Germany would not go to war with Poland, giving the world the impression that he was a peaceful leader.

In March 1935, however, Hitler began rearming and introduced compulsory military service, even though this broke the Treaty of Versailles. At that time, he was constantly suffering from stomach cramps and also developed a sore throat—the result of giving hundreds of speeches. Hitler was certain he had cancer as his mother had. On May 23, 1935, surgeons removed a small growth from his throat, which proved to be benign (harmless). Hitler was advised not to shout or scream when making speeches, something he found difficult to do.

In June 1935, Hitler signed a treaty with the British that said Germany could build a navy one-third the size of Britain's, including submarines.

## Italy invades Abyssinia

In October 1935, the Italian dictator Benito Mussolini invaded Abyssinia (now Ethiopia). It was an unprovoked attack by a powerful nation on a defenseless country. Hitler supported Mussolini by providing him with raw materials. In October 1936, the two leaders signed an agreement of political friendship known as the Rome–Berlin **Axis.**

## Hitler reoccupies the Rhineland

Under the Treaty of Versailles, no German troops were allowed in the **Rhineland.** In early 1936, Hitler decided it was time to go against the treaty. His army generals did not agree with his decision and warned Hitler that it could start a war with France and Britain. Hitler ignored them and made plans to send 3,000 troops into the Rhineland on March 7, 1936. The troops were told to withdraw if the French army challenged them. Their advance was timed to coincide with a speech that Hitler was making in the Kroll Opera House in Berlin. For two days the whole of Germany held its breath, waiting for the French and British to tell the Germans to withdraw. However, both countries were more worried about Italy's invasion of Abyssinia, and did nothing to stop Hitler.

▲ Here, Hitler walked with Mussolini (on Hitler's right) in Rome.

▲ *German troops entered the Rhineland on March 7, 1936.*

The Führer was elated. Although he had taken a risk, he had gotten away with it. He spoke on the radio, telling the German people, "that you have me is the miracle of our time, and that I have found you is Germany's fortune." Hitler's popularity soared and his confidence was boosted.

In July 1936, General Francisco Franco rebelled against the Socialist government of Spain and started the **Spanish Civil War.** Franco was a **Fascist** and therefore won the support of Hitler. Hitler sent soldiers and planes from the *Luftwaffe* to help Franco, enabling them to gain experience in fighting. Hitler was getting bolder, and in November 1936, he signed an agreement with Japan in which both countries declared their opposition to **Communism.**

At Christmas 1936, Hitler visited the Berghof. His stomach cramps had continued and he now had eczema, a skin condition, which was so painful he could not wear boots. In desperation he employed a new doctor, Theodor Morell, who prescribed a variety of medicines. Within a month the eczema had cleared up and Hitler expressed his satisfaction with his new doctor. Eva Braun, however, hated Morell, who was overweight and had dirty fingernails. She said he had "the habits of a pig" and refused to visit him.

## *Anschluss* (Union) with Austria

On November 5, 1937, Hitler called a secret meeting with his generals and told them that he aimed to use force to conquer *lebensraum* for Germany. Some of the top generals opposed the use of force, so Hitler dismissed them for their disobedience. On Christmas Eve, Hitler rashly decided to go for a walk around Munich with his servant, Karl Krause. He was thrilled that members of the public had not recognized him, but Himmler, the leader of the **SS,** was furious. If an opponent had recognized the Führer he could have been assassinated.

Hitler was determined to take over Austria, the country of his birth, and make it part of a Greater Germany. In February 1938, the Austrian chancellor, Kurt von Schuschnigg, was invited to meet Hitler at the Berghof. Hitler demanded that Arthur Seyss-Inquart, an Austrian Nazi, become a minister in the Austrian government. A shaken Schuschnigg refused and Hitler lost his temper, issuing orders for troops to gather along the Austrian border to get ready for an invasion. Austrian Nazis then began rioting in the streets of Vienna and, amid the chaos, Hitler called for Schuschnigg to be replaced by Seyss-Inquart as head of government. On March 11, Schuschnigg crumbled under the pressure exerted by Hitler and resigned his post. Seyss-Inquart was appointed chancellor and, on March 12, invited German troops to cross the border and occupy Austria. Hitler followed with his private escort of twelve cars and made a triumphant entry into Linz, where he had attended the local *Realschule* as a teenager.

With tears running down his cheeks, Hitler addressed a crowd of 100,000 wildly cheering Austrians. He then paid an emotional visit to the nearby town of Leonding, where he laid a wreath on his parents' grave. On March 14, Austria was formally joined to Germany, even though the **Treaty of Versailles** had forbidden this.

## Czechoslovakia and the policy of appeasement

Hitler, thrilled about his triumph in Austria, now turned his attention to Czechoslovakia. Over 3 million German-speaking people lived in the Sudetenland, an area of northwest

Czechoslovakia bordering Germany. Hitler claimed the Sudeten Germans were being badly treated by the Czech government and demanded that the Sudetenland should be given to Germany. In the summer of 1938, German troops massed along the border, ready to invade.

◄ A delighted crowd greeted Hitler with the Nazi salute in Linz, Austria, on March 12, 1938.

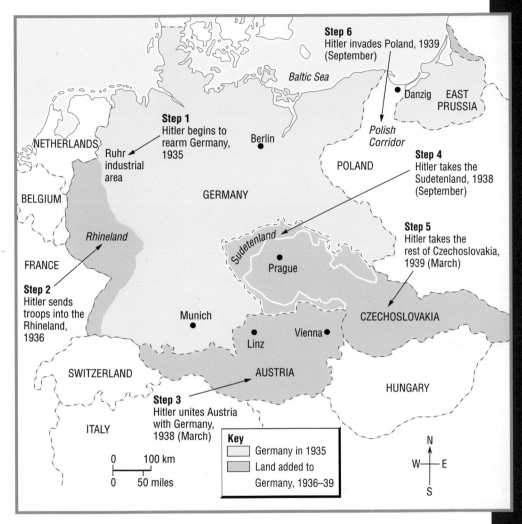

Step 6
Hitler invades Poland, 1939
(September)

Baltic Sea

Danzig    EAST
          PRUSSIA

Step 1
Hitler begins to
rearm Germany,
1935

Berlin

Polish
Corridor

NETHERLANDS

Ruhr
industrial
area

POLAND

Step 4
Hitler takes the
Sudetenland, 1938
(September)

BELGIUM

GERMANY

Rhineland

Step 5
Hitler takes the
rest of Czechoslovakia,
1939 (March)

FRANCE

Sudetenland

Prague

Step 2
Hitler sends
troops into the
Rhineland,
1936

Munich

CZECHOSLOVAKIA

Vienna

Linz

SWITZERLAND

AUSTRIA

HUNGARY

Step 3
Hitler unites Austria
with Germany,
1938 (March)

ITALY

Key

0    100 km

Germany in 1935

0    50 miles

Land added to
Germany, 1936–39

N
W    E
S

▲ *This map illustrates the steps leading to World War II in 1935–39.*

Neville Chamberlain, the British Prime Minister, believed in
appeasement; he was prepared to consider Hitler's demands
in order to avoid war. At a conference in Munich from
September 28 to September 30, 1938, Britain and France
agreed that the Sudetenland should be given to Germany if
Hitler promised to take no more territory. The Czechs were
not even consulted, but they had to accept the agreement or
fight Germany alone. They felt cheated and betrayed.

## The outbreak of war

Chamberlain announced that the Munich agreement had brought "peace in our time." But in March 1939, German troops were sent to occupy the rest of Czechoslovakia. It was now clear that Hitler could not be trusted, and Britain and France prepared for war. In the same month, Hitler took the city of Memel in Lithuania and demanded that Danzig, a port on the Baltic Sea taken from Germany by the **Treaty of Versailles,** be given back. On August 24, 1939, the world was shocked to learn that Germany had signed the Nazi–Soviet Pact with the **USSR.** Although Hitler hated both **Communism** and the USSR, this agreement meant he could wage war in western Europe without being attacked by the Soviets in the east. Hitler also secretly agreed with Joseph Stalin, the Soviet leader, that Germany and the USSR would split Poland between them.

On September 1, 1939, German troops attacked Poland. Britain had promised to help the Poles if they were invaded, and a message was sent to Hitler telling him to withdraw his troops. He did not reply, and on September 3, Britain and France declared war on Germany. World War II had started.

# The War Leader

On September 1, 1939, Hitler launched a **blitzkrieg** attack on Poland. Swiftly moving tanks, supported by dive-bombers, paratroopers, and **infantry,** ripped through the Polish defenses, and by the end of the month Poland had been conquered. The French had originally devised blitzkrieg tactics in 1934, but Hitler adopted the idea and used it with great success. In April and May 1940, Hitler used the same tactics to overrun Denmark, Norway, the Netherlands, Belgium, and Luxembourg. German forces then swept into France and, by June 14, had captured Paris. So far everything was going right for Hitler. He took great delight in going on a three-hour sightseeing tour of the occupied city, taking in the Eiffel Tower and Napoleon's tomb. The Führer admitted that he was "fascinated" by the wonderful architecture of the French capital.

▲ Hitler, accompanied by army generals, visited the Eiffel Tower in Paris on June 25, 1940.

## The Battle of Britain

Hitler's success led him to believe that he was a military genius who could do no wrong. He dominated meetings with his army generals, making all the major tactical decisions.

Hitler's next goal was to invade Britain. To do this he needed to have control of the skies over the English Channel. The Battle of Britain, which began in July 1940, was the first battle ever fought to control the air. Throughout August and September 1940, the **Luftwaffe** attacked factories and airfields in southern England, using bombers supported by Messerschmitt fighters. The *Luftwaffe* was confronted by **RAF** Spitfire and Hurricane fighters, whose pilots shot down over 1,700 German planes. Hitler realized that the *Luftwaffe* could not withstand such heavy losses and called off the invasion.

## Hitler invades the USSR

On June 22, 1941, Hitler broke the Nazi–Soviet Pact and ordered German forces to invade the **USSR.** His aim was to win **lebensraum** and capture the huge Soviet oil fields. Things went well at first, and by early December, German troops had reached the outskirts of Leningrad and Moscow. But the **Red Army** halted their advance, and the Germans found themselves stranded in their summer uniforms in the middle of the freezing Soviet winter. By now Hitler had established his military headquarters at the Wolfsschanze ("Wolf's Lair"), in a forest near Rastenburg in eastern Germany. He brought with him his personal secretary and his Alsatian dog, Blondi. Hitler often interrupted long meetings with his generals to teach Blondi tricks and walk her in the woods.

On December 7, 1941, the Japanese launched an unprovoked attack on Pearl Harbor, an American naval base on the Hawaiian Islands. The following day, United States President Franklin Roosevelt declared war on Japan. On December 11, a confident Hitler showed his support for the Japanese by declaring war on the U.S. It was to prove to be a crucial error. Germany was now at war with the U.S. and the USSR, potentially the two most powerful countries in the world.

## The final solution

As the German army pushed eastward into the USSR, specially trained **SS** action groups followed behind. Their task was to round up Jewish people, shoot them, and bury them in mass graves. At a conference in Berlin in January 1942, the Nazis agreed on the final solution to the Jewish "problem": all the Jews in Europe were to be exterminated. Although Hitler was not at the conference, he gave the go-ahead for Jews to be transported to **extermination camps,** such as Auschwitz in southern Poland, where they were gassed to death with cyanide.

In early November 1942, the Germans were defeated by the British at the battle of **El Alamein** in North Africa. Before this, Hitler had ordered the German army, under General von Paulus, to attack the city of Stalingrad. Soviet troops defended Stalingrad bravely and, in January 1943, launched a counter-attack. Von Paulus, defying Hitler's orders to fight on in a hopeless situation, surrendered. From now on Hitler was in retreat, and his fortunes began to decline rapidly.

▲ The German army retreated from Stalingrad in February 1943. The Germans lost almost 200,000 men in the battle and never recovered.

## Hitler's ailing health

The pressure of war started to take its toll on Hitler. He suffered a long bout of flu and complained of severe headaches. Hitler still had stomach cramps and had great difficulty sleeping. Dr. Morell prescribed over twenty drugs, including hormone injections. The Führer was convinced that the drugs were curing him, but it is more likely that they were poisoning his body. For days on end he stayed alone in his room in the Wolfsschanze with only Blondi for company. He was in a state of depression and his ability to think clearly was impaired. Decisions that needed to be made quickly were delayed as the war turned in favor of the **Allies.**

Hitler's visits to Berlin became rare. He was becoming detached from the German people and rapidly losing popularity. Many of Hitler's generals were turning against him. They could see that defeat was close. Field Marshal Milch told Hitler to take Germany out of the war, but his advice was ignored. On March 13, 1943, a group of generals tried to assassinate Hitler. A bomb was planted on the plane taking him to the Wolfsschanze. It failed to explode and the plane landed safely.

In April 1943, Hitler traveled south for a break at the Berghof. His daily routine here remained much the same as it had been in the 1930s. As usual, Hitler lunched in mid-afternoon before taking a walk. The evening was spent watching movies, after which Hitler talked for hours. He droned on about his childhood, his days in Vienna, and his experiences during World War I. He was still a vegetarian and told his guests that "the elephant is the strongest animal; he also cannot stand meat." His diet consisted of thick gruel, oatmeal soup, and baked potatoes soaked in linseed oil. Eva Braun was still kept out of the limelight, although on one occasion Hitler gave her a public lecture on the evils of smoking.

# D-Day, June 6, 1944

As the **Red Army** pushed the Germans westward out of the **USSR,** the killing of Jewish people was sped up. In January 1944, Himmler, head of the **SS,** boasted that 6 million Jews had already been killed. In the Pacific Ocean, American and Australian troops were pushing the Japanese back. In Europe, Hitler was aware that an invasion of France by American and British forces was definitely coming.

Just after midnight on June 6, 1944 (D-Day), Allied troops landed on the beaches of Normandy in northern France. Hitler was staying at the Berghof and was woken up at 9:00 A.M. to be told the bad news. The Germans had been caught off guard. But Hitler took the news of the invasion remarkably lightly, and declared that the German army would destroy the invaders.

▲ *These American troops landed on a Normandy beach in June 1944. The Allies' task was to drive the Germans eastward out of France.*

## The army bomb plot

Hitler, at 51 years old, was now suffering from **jaundice** on top of all his other illnesses. He was walking with a stoop and visibly aging. Opposition to Hitler within the German army was growing. On July 20, 1944, Lt. Colonel Count Claus von Stauffenberg and a group of army officers hatched a plot to murder Hitler. Summoned to a meeting at the Wolfsschanze, Stauffenberg put a bomb in his briefcase before entering the conference room. Once inside he placed the briefcase under the table as close to Hitler as he could. Stauffenberg left the room on the pretext of making a telephone call, and minutes later the bomb went off. Hitler miraculously escaped the full blast of the bomb and survived. He had burns on his leg, his right arm was partly paralyzed, and his eardrums were damaged. Afterward, Hitler took his revenge and had almost 200 people killed for their part in the plot. Stauffenberg was executed on the same day. Hitler had been badly shaken, but the fact that he survived led him to believe that fate meant him to win the war.

By the end of 1944, however, Germany was on the brink of defeat in Europe. The Americans and British had swept through France and were closing in on Germany. At the same time, the **Red Army** was advancing on Germany from the east. In December the Germans launched a counterattack with an army mainly made up of 16-year-olds in the Ardennes, a hilly region spanning eastern France, Luxembourg, and southern Belgium. They won back some ground, but this merely served to delay the now inevitable defeat of Hitler and his regime.

▲ By chance, Mussolini had been due to visit Hitler at the Wolfsschanze ("Wolf's Lair") on the same day as the bomb plot took place. Here, Hitler shows Mussolini the ruins of the Wolfsschanze. The fact that the windows were open at the time helped to lessen the impact of the bomb.

# 11 The Final Months

Starting around 1943, Hitler made fewer and fewer speeches and, as a result, lost his grip on the now demoralized German people. In the final three months of his life, Hitler's physical and mental health deteriorated greatly, and he hardly left the **Chancellery.** On January 30, 1945, Hitler made his final radio broadcast to the German nation. Defiant, he said that the "crisis" would be "mastered [by] our readiness for sacrifice." He issued orders that the German armies should keep on fighting to the end.

▲ *Hitler inspected a unit of the Hitler Youth in the garden of the Chancellery in March 1945. This was one of the last photographs taken of the ailing Führer.*

## Germany invaded

The **Red Army** invaded Germany from the east at the end of January and, in early March, British and American troops crossed the Rhine River and moved toward Berlin. On April 21, Hitler received news that Soviet troops were on the outskirts of Berlin. Together with Eva and his personal staff, he retired to a bunker 52 feet (16 meters) beneath the Chancellery building. Berlin, now defended only by a mixed army of **SS** officers and **Hitler Youth,** came under heavy fire.

## Suicide

On April 28, Hitler dictated his last will and testament. He said he had never wanted a war and, as usual, blamed everything on the Jews. There was not one word of regret or remorse in his testament. Hitler finally married the loyal Eva Braun on April 29. After lunch on April 30, Hitler and Eva retired to their private quarters. At 3:30 P.M. a gunshot rang out. Members of Hitler's staff found both Eva and Hitler dead. She had poisoned herself, and Hitler had shot himself in the mouth after swallowing a cyanide capsule. Their bodies were soaked in gasoline and burned, and the charred remains were buried in the Chancellery garden. On May 7, 1945, the Germans surrendered to bring the war to an end.

### Admiral Karl Dönitz (1891–1981)

Karl Dönitz was the head of the German **U-boat** service during World War II. Just before he died, Hitler named Dönitz as his successor. Dönitz set up his own government and ran Germany for exactly 23 days. He was captured by the British on May 23, 1945, and put on trial for **war crimes** at Nuremberg in 1946. He was found guilty of sinking neutral ships and sentenced to ten years' imprisonment in Spandau prison, Berlin.

# 12 Hitler's Destructive Legacy

Adolf Hitler was the Nazi **dictator** of Germany for just twelve years, from 1933 to 1945. His beliefs, prejudices, and ambition resulted in disaster for Germany and left a long-lasting destructive legacy for millions of people throughout the world.

## Hitler's shadow

*"Hitler's shadow lay over Germany and indeed Europe long after his death. To some extent it still does, and certainly the name continues to evoke passions . . . [Hitler] is still a focus of fear, fascination, and even incredulity, years after his death in the Berlin bunker."*

(The view of John Laver, a British historian, writing in 1997)

## Destruction

Hitler's burning desire to destroy the **Treaty of Versailles,** create a powerful Greater Germany, and conquer *lebensraum* were major factors in bringing about the outbreak of World War II in 1939. The war resulted in the widespread destruction of factories, farms, roads, railways, and homes both in Europe and Asia. There was a huge loss of life: over 15 million soldiers were killed, but some 35 million civilians also perished, including 20 million Soviet citizens. Many of these deaths could have been avoided if Hitler had not chosen to prolong the war by refusing to surrender earlier.

## Germany and Europe divided

Hitler had aimed to create a powerful Greater Germany but, instead, the wartime **Allies** now occupied Germany. They divided Germany into four zones, with each country administering one zone. The capital city, Berlin, was similarly divided into four sectors of occupation. In 1949, Germany was split into two entirely separate countries, a situation that lasted until 1990 (see map on page 54).

Hitler intended to destroy the **USSR** when he invaded in 1941, but instead the USSR emerged from the war as a **superpower.** The **Red Army** overwhelmed the Germans, and as it advanced on Germany in 1944–45, it established communist governments in the countries it liberated. The U.S. and Britain believed that the Soviets were deliberately trying to spread **Communism** and, as a result, Europe became divided between the democratic West and the communist East. A mood of intense distrust and suspicion, known as the **Cold War,** developed between the two sides and lasted until 1991.

▲ *German refugees returned to a devastated Berlin in August 1945.*

**Key**

— The "Iron Curtain" divided the communist East from the democratic West

→ Advance of the Red Army, 1944–45

▨ Communist countries controlled by the USSR

▨ Communist country not controlled by the USSR

**BERLIN**

FRENCH SECTOR

WEST — BRITISH SECTOR  SOVIET SECTOR — EAST

U.S. SECTOR

N
W—E
S

0    500 km
0    300 miles

NORWAY

SWEDEN

North Sea

DENMARK

Baltic Sea

USSR

BRITAIN

NETH.    1

BELGIUM

GERMANY    4    Berlin    POLAND

LUX.    2

FRANCE    3    CZECHOSLOVAKIA

SWITZERLAND    AUSTRIA    HUNGARY

ITALY    YUGOSLAVIA    ROMANIA

Black Sea

BULGARIA

Mediterranean Sea

ALBANIA

GREECE    TURKEY

- In 1945 Germany was divided into four zones of occupation:
  **1** British zone  **2** French zone  **3** American zone  **4** Soviet zone.
- In 1949 zones 1, 2, and 3 were joined to make the democratic country of West Germany. Zone 4 became the communist country of East Germany.
- In 1945 Berlin was divided into 4 sectors of occupation.
- In 1961 the Berlin Wall was built by the East Germans to stop people moving from East Berlin to West Berlin. The wall did not come down until 1989.

▲ This map illustrates the division of Germany and Europe from 1945 to 1990.

## Neo-Nazis

Today, the ghost of Hitler haunts society in the form of "neo-Nazi" groups. Taking Hitler as their "role model," such groups carry out racist attacks on ethnic minorities. Between 1990 and 2000, for example, there were hundreds of attacks on foreigners living in Germany, and 30 foreigners were killed by neo-Nazis. Similar groups are also found in many other countries, including the U.S., Russia, Britain, the Netherlands, and France, despite the efforts of governments to limit their activities.

▲ German civilians and police acting under the Allied military government were forced to file past bodies of Jews from a concentration camp in 1945.

## Memories of the Holocaust

Historians refer to the persecution and mass murder of Jews by Hitler's regime as the Holocaust. When 21 leading Nazis were put on trial at Nuremberg in 1945–46, a detailed picture emerged of how 6 million Jews were murdered in Nazi **extermination camps** during the war. There was huge sympathy for the Jews as a result of the way they had been treated by Hitler. Thousands of surviving Jews flocked to Palestine and reclaimed it as their homeland. Jews had lived in Palestine 2,000 years before, but were expelled by the occupying Romans. Following this, in the seventh century A.D., the Arabs took over Palestine. In 1948, Palestine was split in two. Land was taken from the Arabs and given to the Jews, who declared the state of Israel. Since then, there have been repeated Arab–Israeli wars over disputed territories, and the division between the two groups of people shows few signs of narrowing even today.

## A subject of debate

Arguments about Hitler's role in history still rage on. Many historians believe that Hitler planned to start World War II, but others disagree and argue that Hitler was just an opportunist who took advantage of events as they unfolded. It seems clear that the harsh treatment of Germany after World War I was a powerful contributing factor toward further hostility in Europe. The actions, and lack of action in some cases, of the Western powers once Hitler gained control of Germany also played a part in defining the character of World War II. However, William Shirer, an American journalist, has said of Hitler: "It is true that he found in the German people a natural instrument which he was able to shape to his own sinister ends. But without Adolf Hitler, who was possessed of a demonic personality, uncanny instincts, a cold ruthlessness . . . there almost certainly would never have been a Third Reich."

Hitler's evil deeds and his role in bringing European civilization to the brink of collapse will never be forgotten, and this will remain his most enduring legacy.

# Timeline

**1889** Adolf Hitler is born at Braunau-am-Inn, Austria.

**1900** Hitler attends the *Realschule* in Linz.

**1905** Hitler leaves school.

**1907** Hitler moves to Vienna and fails to gain entrance to the Vienna Academy of Arts.

**1908** Hitler fails with second application to the Vienna Academy of Arts.

**1909–13** Hitler lives in a hostel in Vienna selling painted postcards.

**1913** Hitler moves to Munich in Bavaria, southern Germany.

**1914** World War I begins. Hitler joins the German army and wins the Iron Cross, Second Class.

**1918** Hitler wins the Iron Cross, First Class. Kaiser Wilhelm II abdicates and Germany becomes a republic. Germany surrenders, ending World War I.

**1919** German Workers' Party (DAP) is formed by Drexler. The new democratic German **Reichstag** meets in **Weimar.** Germany signs the **Treaty of Versailles.** Hitler joins the DAP.

**1920** The DAP changes its name to the National Socialist German Workers' Party (Nazi Party).

**1921** Hitler becomes the leader of the Nazi Party and forms the SA.

**1923** French and Belgian troops occupy the Ruhr (January). Germany suffers hyperinflation. Hitler leads the Munich *putsch* in an attempt to overthrow the Weimar government.

**1924** Hitler goes on trial and is sentenced to five years in prison, where he dictates *Mein Kampf.* He is released in December.

**1924–29** Germany experiences a period of prosperity under Gustav Stresemann. The Nazi Party has a low profile.

**1925** The **SS,** Hitler's personal bodyguard, is formed.

**1928** The Nazi Party wins twelve seats in the Reichstag elections.

**1929** The collapse of the American **stock market** in New York starts the **Great Depression.** Hitler meets Eva Braun.

**1930** The Nazi Party wins 107 seats in the Reichstag elections.

**1932** Hitler becomes a German citizen and runs for the presidency, but loses to Paul von Hindenburg. The Nazi Party becomes the largest single party in the Reichstag, winning 230 seats in the July elections.

**1933** Hitler is appointed chancellor of Germany. The Reichstag building catches fire. The Enabling Act is passed, giving Hitler the power to make laws.

**1934** During the "Night of the Long Knives," leading members of the SA are murdered on Hitler's orders. President Hindenburg dies and Hitler declares himself Führer (leader) of Germany.

**1935** Hitler begins to rearm Germany in defiance of the **Treaty of Versailles.** The Nuremberg Laws against the Jews are announced. Mussolini, the Italian dictator, invades Abyssinia.

**1936** Hitler sends troops into the **Rhineland.** The **Spanish Civil War** begins. Berlin hosts the Olympics. Hitler and Mussolini sign the Rome–Berlin **Axis.** Hitler signs an anti-communist alliance with Japan.

**1937** Hitler makes secret plans to use force to conquer *lebensraum* in Austria and Czechoslovakia.

**1938** *Anschluss* (Union): Hitler joins Austria to Germany. Germany occupies the Sudetenland (Czechoslovakia). Jewish businesses and **synagogues** are attacked in the "Night of Crystal Glass."

**1939** Germany occupies the rest of Czechoslovakia. Germany and the **USSR** sign the Nazi–Soviet Pact. Hitler invades Poland using **blitzkrieg** tactics. Britain and France declare war on Germany.

**1940** German troops overrun Denmark, Norway, the Netherlands, Luxembourg, Belgium, and France. The *Luftwaffe* is defeated by the British Royal Air Force in the Battle of Britain. Hitler calls off his planned invasion of Britain.

**1941** Hitler orders the invasion of the USSR. Japan attacks Pearl Harbor; Hitler declares war on the U.S.

**1942** At the Wannsee Conference the Nazis agree on the "final solution"—the mass murder of all Jews in Europe.

**1943** The Germans lose the Battle of Stalingrad.

**1944** Soviet troops push the retreating German army back into Poland. On D-Day, Allied forces invade Normandy in northern France. Army bomb plot to assassinate Hitler fails.

**1945** Hitler marries Eva Braun in his Berlin bunker and they commit suicide the following day. Germany surrenders. The U.S. drops atomic bombs on the Japanese cities of Hiroshima and Nagasaki.

**1945–91** These are the years of the **Cold War.**

**1949** Germany is divided into two separate countries: West Germany (a **democracy**) and East Germany (communist).

**1990** The reunification of Germany takes place.

# Germany under the Nazis

From 1933 to 1945, Germany was a one-man, one-party dictatorship. There were no multi-party elections in Germany after 1933. The Nazi Party was the only political party allowed.

**THE FÜHRER: Adolf Hitler**
"The final authority on all matters."

All government ministers were Nazis.

The Reichstag was used as a "rubber stamp" for Hitler's laws.

## CONTROL

**The SS** (Protection Squad)
- headed by Heinrich Himmler
- "removed" all opposition
- ran the Gestapo (secret police)
- controlled concentration camps
- organized the mass murder of the Jews

**The People's Court**
- headed by Roland Freisler, "the hanging judge"
- tried people for "crimes against the people"

**The Army**
- Hitler was the commander-in-chief.
- Swore an oath of personal loyalty to Hitler (not Germany)

## PROPAGANDA

**Ministry of Popular Enlightenment and Propaganda**
- headed by Joseph Goebbels
- used radio, movies, the arts, and music to brainwash the German people with Nazi ideas
- organized torchlight parades and huge rallies to show off the strength of the Nazis
- censored newspapers that opposed the Nazis

**Nazi Social Groups / Organizations**
- The German Labor front controlled employees and workers (trade unions were banned).
- Joining the Hitler Youth was made mandatory.
- The school curriculum was changed to contain Nazi ideas. The Nazi Teachers' League was formed.
- The Nazi Women's Front taught that women should stay at home and bear "children for the Nazi state."

**The Nazis controlled all aspects of life in Germany**

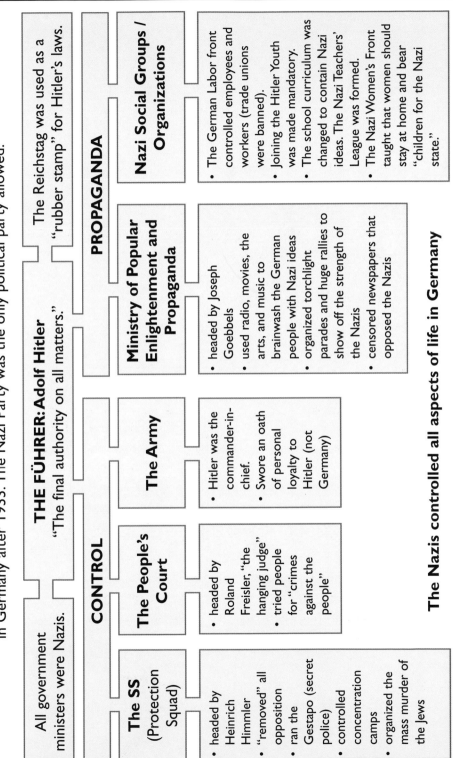

# Sources for Further Research

Altman, Linda J. *The Holocaust, Hitler and Nazi Germany.* Berkeley Heights, N.J.: Enslow Publishers, 1999.

Ayer, Eleanor H. *Adolf Hitler.* San Diego, Calif.: Lucent Books, 1996.

Downing, David. *Benito Mussolini.* Chicago: Heinemann Library, 2001.

Downing, David. *Joseph Stalin.* Chicago: Heinemann Library, 2001.

Freeman, Charles. *The Rise of the Nazis.* Austin, Tex.: Raintree Steck-Vaughn, 1998.

Overy, Richard. *The Penguin Historical Atlas of the Third Reich,* New York: Viking Penguin, 1997.

Reynoldson, Fiona. *Key Battles of World War II.* Chicago: Heinemann Library, 2001.

Stewart, Gail B. *Hitler's Reich.* San Diego, Calif.: Lucent Books, 1994.

Tames, Richard. *Adolf Hitler (Heinemann Profiles Series).* Chicago: Heinemann Library, 1999.

Whittock, Martyn. *Hitler and National Socialism (Heinemann History Through Sources Series).* Chicago: Heinemann Library, 1997.

Willoughby, Susan. *The Holocaust.* Chicago: Heinemann Library, 2001.

# Glossary

**Allies** countries that joined together to fight a common enemy in World War II. The U.S., the USSR, Britain, Australia, New Zealand, and France were commonly referred to as the Allies.

**anti-Semitic** unfounded hostility toward, and prejudice against, the Jewish people

**armistice** agreement between two sides to stop fighting, so that they can draw up a peace treaty

**Aryan** according to Nazi belief, a group of intelligent, physically strong, blond-haired people with no Jewish blood, who were descended from an ancient race

**Axis** word used to describe the partnership of Germany, Italy, and Japan. The Axis powers opposed the Allies during World War II.

**blitzkrieg** German word meaning "lightning war." Attacks were conducted with great speed and force.

**boycott** avoid or refuse to deal with something or someone, such as a country or a store

**Chancellery** collection of government buildings in Berlin

**Cold War** period of tension, hostility, and suspicion between the U.S. and the USSR and their respective allies. Lasting from 1945 to 1991, the Cold War involved the use of threats, spying, propaganda, and military buildup. The U.S. and the USSR never used military weapons directly against each other.

**Communism** system of government where there is no private ownership or social classes, and the government owns all means of production (factories, farms, coal mines, oil fields, etc.). A communist is a person who agrees with the ideas of Communism.

**concentration camps** prison camps set up by the Nazis starting in 1933 for the detention of people who expressed opposition to Hitler. Some were later turned into extermination camps, where many innocent people were murdered.

**degenerate** describes something that has grown worse, or is of low moral capacity

**democracy** system of government where people vote for the government of their choice and there is freedom of speech

**deputy** member of the German parliament

**dictator** leader who has absolute power to run a country

**El Alamein** desert battle fought in Egypt in October and November of 1942 in which the British, under Field Marshal Montgomery, defeated the Germans, led by Erwin Rommel

**ethnic group** people who have a shared culture, language, and religion

**extermination camps** death camps, such as Auschwitz and Treblinka, where the Nazis murdered Jews, Slavs, gypsies, and other groups of people

**Fascist** person who wants his or her country to be militarily strong and under the leadership of an absolute ruler, who has the power to make laws without the approval of a congress or parliament

**Great Depression** period of unemployment and poverty from 1929 to 1934 caused by a slump in world trade

**Hitler Youth** Nazi movement for young people between the ages of 10 and 21

**infantry** soldiers traveling and fighting on foot

**jaundice** yellowing of the skin caused by too much bile in the bloodstream

**League of Nations** international body formed in 1920 to keep world peace and deal with disputes between countries. It was based in Geneva, Switzerland. The U.S. and the USSR refused to join the League of Nations, and Germany was not allowed to join until 1926.

*lebensraum* German word meaning "living space"

*Luftwaffe* German air force

**mutiny** rebellion by soldiers or sailors

**nationalist** person who has strong feelings of devotion and loyalty for his or her country

**overall majority** when one party has more seats in a legislative body than all the other parties put together

**propaganda** the spreading of information giving only one viewpoint. The Nazis used movies, rallies, and posters to spread their ideas and to damage their enemies.

**RAF** British Royal Air Force

**rally** large crowd of people gathered to listen to a speaker

*Realschule* technical high school in Germany taking students from the age of eleven

**Red Army** the army of the communist USSR

**Reichstag** the German congress or parliament

**reparations** compensation for war damage to buildings, factories, roads, and railways

**Rhineland** strip of German territory just west and east of the Rhine River, which includes the cities of Bonn, Düsseldorf, and Cologne

**scurrilous** vulgar and evil

**Slavs** ethnic grouping comprising Soviet, former Yugoslav, and Polish people

**Spanish Civil War** war fought between 1936 and 1939, when rebels led by Francisco Franco fought the democratic Spanish government. Franco won and set up a Fascist dictatorship in Spain that lasted until 1975.

**SS** Hitler's personal bodyguard, the *Schutzstaffel*

**state** Germany was divided into areas called states, such as Bavaria and Prussia. Each state had its own government to run local affairs.

**stock market** place where shares in businesses are sold and bought

**superpower** country with massive economic and military strength. The U.S. and the USSR emerged from World War II as superpowers.

**synagogue** Jewish place of worship

**trade union** organization of workers that safeguards wages and working conditions

**treason** crime of betraying one's country

**Treaty of Versailles** settlement signed on June 28, 1919, between the Allied powers and Germany

**tribunal** committee that rules on a certain issue

**U-boat** short for *Unterseeboot,* a German submarine

**USSR** short for Union of Soviet Socialist Republics—also called the Soviet Union

**war crimes** atrocities, such as mass murder of civilians, in times of war

**Weimar** city in Germany where the new German democratic government met in early 1919

**Western Front** line of German and British trenches that stretched almost continuously from the English Channel to Switzerland; the main area of fighting during World War I

# Index